Why Are You So Scared?

Published by
MAGINATION PRESS
An Educational Publishing Foundation Book
American Psychological Association
750 First Street, NE
Washington, DC 20002

For more information about our books, including a complete catalog,
please write to us, call 1-800-374-2721, or visit our website at
www.apa.com/pubs/magination.

Book design by Susan K. White

Printed by Worzalla, Stevens Point, WI

Library of Congress Cataloging-in-Publication Data
Andrews, Beth.
Why are you so scared? : a child's book about parents with PTSD /
by Beth Andrews ; illustrated by Katherine Kirkland.
p. cm.
ISBN-13: 978-1-4338-1045-9 (hardcover)
ISBN-10: 1-4338-1045-X (hardcover)
ISBN-13: 978-1-4338-1044-2 (pbk.)
ISBN-10: 1-4338-1044-1 (pbk.)
1. Post-traumatic stress disorder. I. Kirkland, Katherine. II. Title.

RC552.P67A536 2012
616.85'21—dc22   2011011082

Manufactured in the United States of America
10 9 8 7 6 5 4 3 2 1

Why Are You So Scared?

A CHILD'S BOOK ABOUT PARENTS WITH PTSD

by Beth Andrews, LCSW

illustrated by Katherine Kirkland

M A G I N A T I O N   P R E S S   •   W A S H I N G T O N ,   D C

American Psychological Association

This book is just for you. It's all about a special kind of problem that some moms and dads might get, called Post Traumatic Stress Disorder (or PTSD).

Kids often ask why their parent has PTSD. It happens when a parent has had something very bad and scary happen to them, or they watched something very bad happen to someone else and could not stop it. This could have been just last month or it might have been a very long time ago, way before you were born. The "Post" in PTSD means it happened a while ago.

PTSD is a problem with feelings, especially feeling scared. What happened in the past for your parent makes them too worried or scared about things now.

Parents with PTSD don't feel scared and worried on purpose. They don't want to feel scared all the time, but they can't help it. Their brains play tricks on them, and they might think that things are dangerous now when they are really very safe.

You can't catch PTSD like you can catch a cold. You can't see it like you can see if someone is coughing and has a runny nose. A grown-up might look fine on the outside, but just feel really bad and scared inside.

Draw a picture here of your parent and you.

Here are some of the things that can happen to a parent to cause PTSD:

Getting hurt badly or attacked by someone else

A bad car accident or plane crash

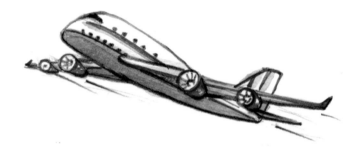

Being in the military
and fighting in a war

Working as a policeman or fireman and getting hurt,
or seeing someone get hurt or die

Being in a tornado, hurricane, fire, flood, or earthquake

Being close by when a bomb goes off

You can ask your parent what happened but they may not be able to talk about it. Or they may want to protect you by not talking too much about it.

Sometimes, parents act different when they have PTSD. They may not be able to sleep or they might have bad nightmares. Then they are very tired and cranky the next day and they might yell or be too tired to play.

They might be really jumpy and get very scared if they see or hear or smell something that reminds them of what happened. They might even not want to go places with you because they are so worried.

Parents with PTSD might have what we call a "flashback." When this happens, they feel like they are back in the bad, scary place again and they might not know that they are here and now and it isn't happening again.

They might be really worried about you all the time and try too hard to protect you by not letting you do things or go places you want to go.

They might have a hard time having happy feelings or having fun with you, or they might act mad or sad most of the time.

They might seem like they are daydreaming a lot or not want to talk to you or hug you.

They may have a hard time paying attention or they may not remember things that are important, like a promise they made to you or when your soccer game is.

Another common thing that can happen is something called a "panic attack." A grown-up gets so scared that they start to sweat, shake, and get dizzy. They might feel sick to their stomach, have pain in their chest, and have a hard time getting their breath.

This can be scary to watch, but people don't die from panic attacks. It will pass in a few minutes and they will be OK again.

Parents with PTSD usually do not do well with sudden loud noises or with people sneaking up behind them and jumping out and surprising them. They won't think this is funny. This is not a loving thing to do and might not be safe for anyone, so it is not a good idea.

It is also not a good idea to try to wake up a parent who is having a nightmare. Since they are asleep, they might think you are part of the dream and accidentally hurt you.

Would you like to draw a picture of your parent here?

Some parents drink too much alcohol or use drugs to try to get rid of the scary feelings. This is not a good way to handle the feelings because it causes lots of other problems.

Sometimes a parent gets so mad that they hit or hurt someone else in the family. If this doesn't happen at your house, you can skip this page. If this does happen in your house or if you don't feel safe, it is important to tell an adult you trust outside your home who can help you. You might pick a teacher or school counselor or a friend's parent. People getting hurt should never be a secret.

There is some good news. There are lots of things that moms and dads can do to help themselves feel better. They might spend time talking with someone called a therapist or counselor. That's a person who has special training on how to help your parent feel better.

They might go to a group of other grown-ups who have the same problems and talk about how they can help each other.

Sometimes a parent might go see a doctor who will give them medicine to help them feel better.

Kids have lots of feelings when their mom or dad gets PTSD.

Do you ever feel like this?

Angry

Scared

Guilty

Lonely

Embarrassed

Sad

Worried

Hurt

Loving

Sometimes kids think it isn't OK to feel certain ways, but you should know that lots of kids have these feelings when a parent has problems. Whatever you are feeling is OK, and sometimes talking about your feelings will help you feel better.

Draw a picture about what you are feeling today.

Sometimes kids worry that the PTSD is their fault. It's important to remember that it is not your fault. It was caused by the bad and scary thing that happened to your parent.

You didn't cause it by anything you did.

Kids might think that they can do something to fix the PTSD. But you can't fix it for your parent by being really good or helpful, or by joking around, or by being naughty, or by anything else you do. Therapists and doctors can help your mom or dad heal their PTSD, but that's not your job. Remember that PTSD is never your fault, but helping with chores is a nice thing to do if you want.

Your job is to be a kid, play, have friends, and do your very best in school. It's OK to have fun and be a kid, even when mom or dad is feeling bad.

What have you tried to do, thinking that you could make it better?

It's important to remember that your mom or dad still love you, even if they have a hard time showing it sometimes. The PTSD can get in the way of showing the love, but that doesn't change their love for you.

You still love your parent, too, even when you feel really mad at them. Did you know that you can love someone and feel angry at them at the same time? When we feel angry, sometimes it is hard to remember that we still love the other person.

It can also help to remember that you are not alone.
Lots of other kids have parents with PTSD.
And there are lots of people who care about you
and your feelings.

Some of these people might be your parents, friends, teachers, aunts and uncles, brothers and sisters, grandparents, other relatives, neighbors, babysitters, people at your church or synagogue, and your friends' parents.

There are things that kids can do to help themselves feel better living with a mom or dad who has PTSD. You can tell your parents how you feel about how they are acting and how it is affecting you. And you can ask for what you need. For example, you can ask them if you need a hug or someone to take you to school or if you are hungry.

If your mom or dad can't give you what you need, you can ask another caring adult you know and trust for help. If you aren't sure who to ask, maybe one of your parents can help with suggestions.

Sometimes kids go and visit a therapist. There they talk, play, and do artwork about the things that are bothering them. Therapists know how to help kids feel better.

Sometimes drawing pictures can help kids feel better.

Here you can draw a picture of your family or your feelings or anything else you want to draw.

Having a parent who has PTSD can be scary and feel pretty bad at times, but you can do things to help yourself feel better. Just remember:

- PTSD is there because your parent had something really bad and scary happen to them.
- They don't want to act this way, but their brain plays tricks on them.
- It's not your fault.
- YOU can't fix it, but there are people who can help your parent.
- It's OK to have whatever feelings you have about this.
- Your parent still loves you, and you still love them.
- There are lots of things you can do to help yourself feel better.

Note To Parents and Other Caregivers

By Bret A. Moore, PsyD, ABPP

Posttraumatic Stress Disorder (PTSD) is an emotionally painful and often disabling condition that affects approximately 8 percent of American adults each year. PTSD occurs following a traumatic event, such as an automobile accident, natural disaster, rape, or exposure to combat. Although PTSD only occurs following a traumatic event, it does not necessarily occur, and not everyone who has experienced trauma develops PTSD. To be diagnosed with PTSD, the person must also react to the experienced event with a sense of fear, helplessness, or horror. He or she may be plagued by nightmares, withdrawal from loved ones, or depression. PTSD is more common in women and combat veterans and it can last a person's entire lifetime.

PTSD can negatively affect the children of parents or caregivers who experience it. In addition to being confused and worried about their parent or caregiver, children may experience fear and sadness of their own. A negatively affected child may suffer poor performance at school, act out at daycare, or withdraw from family and friends. PTSD is not just a condition of the adult, but a condition of the family and others close to the child.

How This Book Can Help

There are several important aspects of their parent or caregiver's PTSD that children should understand. Although your child's age and maturity level, and your own comfort level, should dictate how much emphasis you give any particular issue, it's important that each of the following be acknowledged, at least to plant a seed for future discussion. This book, and the discussions it is meant to facilitate, should help your child:

- understand what PTSD is and what it is not;
- recognize and cope with his or her feelings; and
- realize that things will get better and that help is available.

This book is meant to be read by or to your child with guidance from a parent, teacher, counselor, or other adult that he or she trusts. Although you can accomplish this in several ways, it may be best to read it in sections. This way, several discussions can take place over an extended period, allowing time for your child to form questions and discover his or her own solutions to some of the concerns covered in the book. Regardless of how you decide to use this book, remember to watch for cues from your child. He is the best measure for how much information is too much and when it's OK to keep reading and talking.

Helping Your Child Cope With Parental PTSD

Sitting down with your child and this book is an excellent way to begin. It will answer many questions that your child has, suggest a number of ways to cope, open up communication between parent and child, and give you ideas on how to talk with your child about PTSD. Here are some ongoing ways you can help your child cope with your PTSD.

Listen to your child. The most important thing you can do as a parent or caregiver is to listen to your child. Encourage her to share thoughts and feelings, whether they are positive or negative. Refrain from passing judgment or trying to convince your child that she shouldn't feel or think a certain way. Being seen as critical or dismissive will almost always result in the child clamming up and burying their feelings inside.

Help your child identify and name feelings and emotions, and make sure your child knows that it's OK to talk about any feeling with you. Respond in a nonjudgmental way, and communicate your acceptance of whatever feelings emerge—especially the more negative ones, such as anger, worry, and so on. Kids are often reluctant to admit to negative feelings and may deny having them. When this happens, try responding with gentle humor. For example, if you say, "I'll bet you were pretty annoyed when I was not feeling up to going to your soccer game," and your child shrugs and says, "That's okay," you could respond with, "Well, you must be the only kid in the world who wouldn't get angry! I know I would have been hopping mad!"

Use age-appropriate examples. PTSD is a complicated disorder that most adults don't even understand. A great way to help children understand complicated issues is to make age-appropriate comparisons using examples they can relate to. For example, most children have been afraid of monsters at some point. Remind your child how it felt when he first "saw" or imagined a monster in the closet or under the bed. Explain that this is how you felt during a traumatic event. You might say something like, "Just like you'll do anything not to think about a monster under your bed, I try to avoid thinking about what happened to me." Explain that just like your child doesn't like to go under the bed or near the closet, you don't like to go near the place where the trauma occurred. Also, highlight the fact that being scared can cause many problems, such as feeling sad, having bad dreams, and not wanting to go to sleep. If you find that this example doesn't work for your situation, feel free to use one of your own.

Practice caution when giving details of the traumatic event. A child doesn't need to know the most troubling aspects of the incident. Telling the truth about your condition can produce trust and a sense of security; however, it is important that you avoid telling your child more than she needs to know for things to make sense or to calm unwarranted fears. Keep examples and comparisons age appropriate, and remember always to take your cues from your child and listen to her thoughts and feelings when you are discussing your PTSD.

Affirm your love. Remind your child that you love him and always will, even though your actions may sometimes be scary or might not seem very loving. You can also give your assurance that things will get better. Try not to yell at your child or argue with loved ones in his presence, and avoid using your child as a source for your own emotional support. Show support for your child by giving hugs and kisses and saying kind words.

It's not their fault. While it is a good idea to involve the entire family in your healing process, it's important to reassure your child that he or she is not at fault for your PTSD. Although it may seem obvious to you that your child is not to blame, children have a tendency to internalize blame and responsibility for the suffering of loved ones. Also, explain to your child that her job is to not to "fix" the loved one.

The psychological makeup of children is complicated. Even with caring, love, and support, some children will need professional help. Additionally, the best thing you can do for your child might be to get professional help for yourself. If you're not sure where to go, ask for a referral from your family doctor, a counselor at your child's school, your clergyperson, state or local mental health associations, or a friend or neighbor who has had a good treatment experience. Don't look at this as a failure on your part. Look at it as an opportunity to help your child grow and become a stronger person.

—*Bret A. Moore, PsyD, is a former active-duty U.S. Army psychologist and two-tour veteran of Operation Iraqi Freedom. He is the author and editor of several books, publishing most recently an APA Lifetools book with Carrie H. Kennedy, PhD,* Wheels Down: Adjustment to Life After Deployment.

About the Author

Beth Andrews is a licensed clinical social worker, program supervisor for a community mental health center in Colorado, and college instructor. She is the author of two other self-help books for children—*Why Are You So Sad? A Child's Book About Parental Depression* and *I Miss You! A Military Kid's Book About Deployment*.

About the Illustrator

Katherine Kirkland is an illustrator living in the Gloucestershire countryside in England with her husband and son. Katherine illustrates greetings cards and children's books and has always had a passion for drawing.